THE CHARISMA OF ANIMALS

poems by

Gregory Maertz

Finishing Line Press
Georgetown, Kentucky

THE CHARISMA
OF ANIMALS

Copyright © 2023 by Gregory Maertz
ISBN 979-8-88838-233-2 First Edition
All rights reserved under International and Pan-American Copyright Conventions. No part of this book may be reproduced in any manner whatsoever without written permission from the publisher, except in the case of brief quotations embodied in critical articles and reviews.

ACKNOWLEDGMENTS

I wish to express my gratitude to the friends who let themselves be prevailed upon to read early drafts of my poems. Their encouragement inspired me to keep writing.

Publisher: Leah Huete de Maines
Editor: Christen Kincaid
Cover Art: Gregory Maertz
Author Photo: Carl G. Friedrich Photographer
Cover Design: Elizabeth Maines McCleavy

Order online: www.finishinglinepress.com
also available on amazon.com

Author inquiries and mail orders:
Finishing Line Press
P. O. Box 1626
Georgetown, Kentucky 40324
U. S. A.

Table of Contents

The Island of White Horses 1

Riverside Drive 6

Heart Killer 8

Wolf Bitten 9

Adieu to the NHC 10

Gravir 11

Bell Poem 13

Lethe Poem 14

Bergen 15

Moon Poem 16

Molokai 17

Fridge Poem 19

Heidelberg 20

Halstead's Bay 24

Paris 25

Munich 26

Griggstown 27

The Coldest Night 29

Mere Symbols 30

The Morning After 32

Voice of the Stars 33

Heart Poem	34
Time Poem	35
Birth Poem	36
Pinecone Poem	37
Stolen Dog	38
Tree Shadows	39
Biographical Note	40

To my muse

"I've dreamt in my life dreams that have stayed with me ever after, and changed my ideas: They've gone through and through me, like wine through water, and altered the color of my mind."

Emily Brontë

"The true mystery of the world is the visible, not the invisible"

Oscar Wilde

The Island of White Horses

      I

On the island of white horses
The brooding sky darkens the narrow loch
And daubs my windows with silent drops.
The wild-eyed gannets, gliding in urgent arcs,
Plummet to the blue-grey water like falling darts.
And then, with a subtle twist of their wings,
They are hoisted back up into the sky again.

With the earth, sun, and moon perfectly aligned,
The plunging spring tide airs the green foreshore,
Stranding piles of mussels, black as lava rock,
That tempt the otter bitch to leave her hungry romp.

*The narrow loch (fjord) = Loch Odhairn ("Hell Lake" in Scottish Gaelic)
*Romp = litter of otter pups

      II

On the island of white horses
The new morning sun sets
The purple hills ablaze,
Spotlighting a lone red deer stag
In a herd of hinds and calves
Grazing on the ripe heather.

Above them, wheeling between
The fiery towers of clouds,
A pair of buzzards sweeps
Intersecting circles
Around their fledgling chick
Whose mewing kitten cry is
The only sound breaking the silence.

*Buzzard = hawk-sized raptor

III

On the island of white horses,
The easterly wind fans the jade loch
Into an endless rippling stream.
Curtains of mist flutter from the tops
Of the cliffs like sails of phantom ships.

An eerie silence reigns over the fjord
As the meadow pipits cease their song,
And the ewes on the opposing shore
Nuzzle their lambs into submission.

Gradually the sky brightens,
Gashes of blue tear the clouds,
And tiny spotted butterflies
Drift in the suddenly warming air.

IV

On the island of white horses,
Midsummer's eve arrives
On ash-grey heron's wings.
The long-plighted pair from
The heronry below Cromore
Crosses the loch's mirroring
Surface to the southern shore.

An otter fishes below
The ruins of the old salt house,
Porpoising guilelessly in
The icy turquoise shallows.
The cuckoo, its mate's damage done
To a meadow pipit's brood,
Roosts on my chimney, watchful,
Unlovely, but no longer sings.

Haar oozes into the loch
With the scent of the open sea.

As the sun begins its descent
Into winter's dark embrace,
Crystalline pinpricks speckle
The loch's polished veneer.

*Cromore = village a few miles north of Gravir
*Haar = sea fog

V

On the island of white horses,
The stiff westerly breeze has creased
The dark loch into furrows of cerulean and teal.

Three cloudless days in a row have lured
The ewes and lambs grazing beside the old salt house
To climb the rutted peat tracks to the fresh grass aloft.

At the edge of the sky, the grey outcroppings of gneiss
Are draped in plummy swathes of ripening heather.
A giant golden eagle, for the third day in a row,
Orbits the double summit above the ruined croft,
Casting ragged shadows on the waving bracken below.

*Lewisian gneiss = some of the oldest rock on earth

VI

On the island of white horses,
As I trod the moorland track
That curves around Loch nan Faoileag,
A grunting heron scythed overhead.

Then, as I climbed the crest to Highgales,
My croft house snuggled into the steep hillside,
A mottled sea eagle sailed toward me,
Its long dark finger feathers tilling the sky.

Seen from above, the surface of the loch is still,

Broken only by the rictuses of rising mackerel,
And the plashing of a greedy, surging seal.

*Loch nan Faoileag = Loch of the Seagulls, a freshwater lake that lies above Gravir
*Sea eagle = Scotland's largest bird of prey

VII

On the island of white horses,
The first westerly gale of July roars
Through the slender, steep-sided fjord,
Stringing the sheep on the Toum into a skein—
Wavy green velvet knotted with pearls.

The horizontal waterfall of mist, rain, and wind
Breaks against my windows and sturdy front door,
Flinging the riot of seabirds earthward to the shore.
Only a solitary black-back gull braves the air,
Careening wildly on wings half-tucked,
A broken arrow gyring down to the steel-gray loch.

*The Toum = a heather-covered mountain across the fjord from Highgales

VIII

On the island of white horses,
The misty early morning twilight
Has turned the sea loch dark emerald.

Roiling the water in isolated pools,
The silver green mackerel are
Shadowed by hovering gulls
And submarined by upsurging seals.

The haar, bringer of silence, seeps
Over the lips of the sheltering hills,
Reducing the world to this inland sea.
An interloping cuckoo, the last to leave,
Pierces the air with an uncanny farewell.

Riverside Drive

She and her sister were deposited at my studio door
By a wave bearing the detritus of divorce,
Black silhouettes darting between the piles of things.

She, the weasel-faced one, was gravely ill,
A bony rabbit skin that purred against my chest at night.
Her foxy-faced sister continued her feral ways,
And always hovered just out of reach.

The hippie vet on Columbus Avenue saved her life.
Within a few weeks, she was sleek and plump,
Playful and ornery,
Purring against my chest at night.
Her sister, wild as always,
Stared with mild astonishment from behind the couch.

We had two years of a shared life together,
Never easy in such a small space, but happy.

Then, suddenly, she began bleeding
Explosively from her ears and nose.
She stopped purring against my chest at night
And chose to sleep on a makeshift bed in the closet.

This time the kind doctor with the ring in his ear
Performed no miracle cure.
I called the ex—not to ask permission—
She had been mine for two years—
But to assuage my grief.

There was little sleep the night before.
There were bad dreams.
In the one that I remember
She was torn from my arms by floodwaters
Near the old house where we once had lived.

Morning brought the ex to my door and
We took her out in her crate and climbed into a cab.

An hour later all that lay between her
And the cold steel table was an old towel.
I sobbed into her soft black fur
As the lethal dose went into a vein on her hind leg.
Her tiny body stiffened, relaxed, and, within minutes, grew cold.
Urine spilled onto the steel table, mixing with my tears.
Bundled up in the towel,
She vanished behind a matte grey door.

Months have passed since then, but
Even now I keep expecting her weasel face
To emerge from around every corner,
To feel her purring against my chest at night.
But there she sits on my bookshelf,
A handful of dust in a plastic jar,
While her feral sister glowers at me
From under the bed.

Heart Killer

One morning I awoke to find
A bloody puddle in my sheets.
Wincing in the mirror, I felt
The entry wound of a spear.

As Bernini's Saint Teresa teaches us,
A heart with a hole will burn and bleed,
And no rapture or ecstasy can quell
Even the purest heart's hunger for its killer.

Then I recalled that before falling
Into a restive, dream-tossed sleep,
The thunderbolt that pierced
My breast was tinted hazel green.

The Ecstasy of St. Teresa (1647-1652) = sculptural ensemble by Gian Lorenzo Bernini (1598-1680) in the church of Santa Maria della Vittoria in Rome

Wolf Bitten

Kissed by the tooth of the lithe she-wolf,
The shy creature that stole into my hearth
And glowers by the fire, just beyond my reach,
I fell into bed to tend to my wounded throat.

As I lay awake under the warming eiderdown,
Either in a trance brought on by her feral gleam
Or a blood-fever imbued by her scarlet mouth,

I caught her savage scent lingering in the sheets.
Breathing it in caused my infected heart to flutter.

Adieu to the NHC

Driving north from Raleigh on I-85,
Under a rising crescent moon,
Each jarring moment in my rattling
Old car brings me closer to you.

Crossing the Virginia state line,
The slice of moon has set, and
With the twilight sky darkening,
Spectral figures are lining the road:

Are they merely hungry deer
Grazing on the grassy verges?
Or forlorn creatures such as I,
Enchanted by hazel green eyes?

Gravir

On this clear moon-swept night
The salty, heathered air
Is alive with sounds.

A lonely cockerel rouses
The slumbering moorscape
With a tentative stutter.
At the far end of the village,
A collie dog offers a muffled woof in reply.

The waterfall above the southern shore
Hisses, purrs, and growls.
Hidden in an overgrown croft,
A corncrake sings like a weird machine,
And invisible lambs bleat in the bracken.

A rising king tide overtops the fishing pier.
Boats strain at their drowning buoys.
Yearling mackerel, argent flakes
Glittering in the stark moonlight,
Spill out of the sea surge onto
The shoreline-hugging, single-track village road.

Now, at this enchanted hour,
In this ancient stone cottage,
I'm keeping watch on the window seat,
Listening to your sleep-breathing,
The first cries of the cuckoo,
And the keening of the seabirds.

Lying in bed, sedated by jet lag
And a tumbler of whisky,
Your arms and legs forming
A relaxed tangle under the duvet,
You brighten the room as if
You were a glowing candle.

The day won't begin for hours.
Until then, the world will
Be bathed in lilac twilight.
Until then, I'll let you sleep,
Resisting the urge to rouse you
To witness the fiery sunrise.

Bell Poem

Last night I suddenly recalled
What your kisses tasted like—
The familiar hints of coconut,
Licorice, and lemon thyme.

In the zebraed darkness you lay
Under the duvet, gently alive.
Indistinctly, I heard you murmur
Like a bell trilling under water.

As I touched your hand, your soft
Fingertips fluttered against my wrist
Like the wings of a small captive bird.

I reached for you, caressed your hip,
And scented your breath as you sighed.
Then I realized that you were dreaming.

Lethe Poem

Oh, no, do not, young Keats implored, to Lethe go.
Do not forget but "glut thy sorrow on a morning rose."   *"Ode on Melancholy" (1819)
You must feed deep, deep upon your lover's angry eyes,
For they, Keats knew, who hurt the most are most alive.

It's too late to invoke Bob Herrick or the Stones' horses wild,
It's too late to pander to the feckless infant god of love.
For once lost, our hearts are no longer ours to rule or guide,
And we become prey to the whims of the bright stars above.

So, in your presence, my love, I am whole, entire, complete,
Recognizing in you the Aristophanic twin I knew at birth.
But in your absence, delicious pain becomes the element
In which I learn to live, love, and, without grieving, hurt.

*John Keats (1795-1821) = English Romantic poet who died tragically young
*Robert Herrick (1591-1674) = quintessential carpe diem English poet
*The Rolling Stones, "Wild Horses," *Sticky Fingers* (1971)
*Aristophanic twin = one's missing double; alluded to in Plato's *Symposium*

Bergen

Last night I dreamed that on my way to see you
I got lost and found myself alone in a castle
In northern Italy, perhaps, or possibly Bavaria.

In a resolute but fruitless search for writing paper
I rummage through the many ornate rooms,
With murals or tapestries adorning the walls
And priceless furniture—tasseled canopy beds and rococo secretaries—
Roped off from too curious children.

I panic and begin scribbling messages to you in hieroglyphs
On antique carpets with a permanent black marker.

Ashamed of my reckless vandalism,
I escape through an upper-story window,
Catching hand- and footholds in the crevices
Of the outer stone wall berobed with vining roses.

As I inch downwards, my lips brush open
The mouths of the ripening blossoms.
Looking down to the ground,
With none of the familiar vertigo,
I realize that I am actually in Bergen,

For, waiting below, is my old acquaintance,
The Norwegian Forest cat, with fur matted and unkempt,
Snatching some warmth on the hood of a car.

I awake in my old house beside Cider Creek
With its freshly painted walls, sweet well water,
And speckled twin fawns prancing in the garden.

It's an hour before sunrise and a thunderstorm is raging.
In the almost tangible darkness, breathing in
The humid, lightning-scented air, I reach for you.

Moon Poem

According to the ordinary sense,
The moon seems absent from the sky.
Fog, night mists, and the aurora
Have obscured the common eye.

But I am in no doubt that
The sacred orb still floats above,
As I can sense its dreadful
Tidal pulling on my blood.

So even now without your love
I can still feel the urgent clasp
Of your lithe fingers evoke
Trembling life from my dormant heart.

Molokai

On the far eastern shore of Molokai,
Below the Shark Tooth Mountains,
Scuttling black coconut crabs,
Sinister shadows sketched by the sun,
Poke holes in the slimy tidal mud.

Just past Mile Marker 18, at the Mana Grocery Store,
The plate lunch special is kalbi with sticky rice.
I add kimchi and a bottle of Maui beer and
Take my picnic to the beach across the road.

The roar of the surf crashing on the distant reef
Comes and goes on the wind like an echo.
Across the frothing channel, Lanai rises like a mirage,
Its cone-shaped volcanic crest draped in ever-present cloud.

Back in the parking lot of the island's only hotel,
A grey ponytailed haole man is babytalking   *haole = "stranger" or Caucasian
To a blonde toddler and a border collie.
The two of them crouch together in a big cage
Loaded in the back of a red pickup.
"Dakota, the girl," he informs no one in particular,
"Was named after Dakota, the dog."

At the hotel bar Pono, the burly fisherman with facial tattoos,
Announces that after chasing the Maui and Oahu boats
Away from the reef, he caught a giant opakapaka.   *Hawaiian red snapper

Andrew, the deeply tanned barman with a twinkling grin,
Matter-of-factly declares that the African antelope
Is back in his pasture. Answering quizzical looks from the tourists,
He explains: "When they closed the Wild Animal Park,
They were supposed to kill the animals, but they let them go."

In cheerful silence I eat my dinner just feet from the water.
The coconut crabs have disappeared into their holes.
Drinking in the pigeon-inflected banter of the restaurant staff—

Combining a familiar tone with verbal gestures of respect—
I am transported to the Hawaii of my childhood.

In the morning, an hour before sunrise, I'm awakened
By a chorus of feral roosters and the lurid howling
Of guinea fowl and peacocks, offspring of other escapees.

Fridge Poem

Today I cleared my whirring fridge
Of all the reminders of you—
The half-eaten nub of butter and
The frozen-lidded raspberry jam
That we smeared on baguettes
Mornings after we made love.

Then I found a stale cube of chocolate—
Dried out, bloomed, and grey—
That I didn't hesitate to drop on my tongue.

The sweet, herby, sour butter tang
Reminded me of how you tasted
When I found your mouth in the dark.

Heidelberg

When we sat down in the garden in Karlsruhe
The swallows appeared punktlich at seven.   *precisely
Their screeching harpy cries
Seemed to announce the end of time.

Then, in another sign of the coming apocalypse,
A blazing white stork swept
The swallows from the darkening sky.
Thunder scattered a fistful of raindrops
And our dinner plates had be rescued.

All eyes turned upwards in wonderment and worry,
But the tempest passed and the bread and wine,
Salvaged from the rain, reappeared on the table.

With twilight came the turn of tiny bats to feed.
They fluttered crazily above our heads
Like drunken nocturnal butterflies.

Other uncanny beasts, spiny, toy-like hedgehogs,
Crept out from the border of flowers
And sipped the milk left for them in saucers.

The anxious keening of dogs in adjacent gardens
Unsealed the door to a realm of forgotten memories.
The surrounding ivy-green walls began to echo
With ghostly murmurs and lightning flashes of recognition
From my first year as a Fulbright Scholar in Heidelberg.

Closing my eyes and taking a sacramental gulp of wine,
It's suddenly 33 years ago and I'm walking my bike
Down the Hauptstrasse, amid the throngs of Japanese tourists,
Past the Holy Ghost Church, to the library of the German Seminar.

My stomach clenches as I overhear
A group of grey-headed Germans chirping nostalgically
About "der gute Hermann," not seeming to mind that

Goering was a chief architect of the Holocaust.

Further on, in the Schachklub,   *chess club
Players with bearded, ascetic faces
Peer intently at their boards,
Straining to divine the future.

Moments later, I lock my bike and take
My old seat in the Harmonie Cinema,
Where I used to go every Tuesday night
Until I learned the dubbed German
Dialogue in *Out of Africa* by heart.

Sustaining my labors with sweet popcorn
And beer swigged out of half-liter bottles,
I deciphered that Streep and Redford's voices
Were replaced by clipped northern accents,
While Brandauer overdubbed his own lines
In the cozy dialect of his native Austria.

Back in the street, I'm transported, Mephisto-style,
To a dinner party in a torchlit Schrebergarten.   *community garden plot
It's late on April 30th, Walpurgisnacht, when
Witches and their familiars rule the night.

In the next allotment, wasted fraternity boys
Toast the future rebirth of Greater Germany.
With right arms upraised, with voices in unison,
They hail the shrieking Bohemian Antichrist.   *reference to Adolf Hitler's
                                                             Austrian origins

Then, in the coolness of the morning,
I'm climbing the secluded Himmelleiter,   *stairway to heaven
Steps hand-carved into the sandstone hillside
In the fragrant woods above the ruined castle.

There, in the heart of the Odenwald,
Crisscrossed by ancient forest paths,
The breeze is nectared with sweet pine,
Peppery cornflowers, and wild blueberry.

Exultant but winded, I inhale
The same air breathed by the old gods,
Goethe and Nietzsche, Gundolf and Jaspers,
Before their overthrow by the Blond Beast.

Suddenly, it's Easter morning 1987,
And I've slipped across the border
Into Alsace without my passport.
With each kilometer infernal omens
Of the coming upheaval multiply.

Deserted villages are defended, on the French side,
By the moldering concrete Maginot Line,
And, on the German, by the overgrown West Wall.
Here vast armies once waited in silence
For the end of the world.

The quaint villages have German names
But all the road signs are in French.
Countless grand chateaux are fading
Into ruin among the festering weeds.
The high mountain meadows are dotted
With cattle and horses reverting
To their primordial avatars, aurochs and tarpans.

The hellish route leads straight to Colmar,
Beloved city of Charles the Fat,   *Carolingian Emperor (881-888 CE)
Renowned for its wine festivals, gastronomy,
And perfectly preserved medieval buildings.

Following lunch at the fabled Schillinger's,
Which cost more than my monthly stipend,
I find my way alone to the Isenheim Altarpiece.

*Friedrich Gundolf (1880-1931) = German Jewish poet and literary scholar
*Karl Jaspers (1883-1969) = German philosopher based at the Uni-Heidelberg with Gundolf
*Blond Beast = Nietzsche's metaphor for the "master race," which was exploited by the Nazis

So different from the pretty pictures in Rome and Florence,
In Grünewald's tableau of terrible suffering,
Painted in gangrenous hues with open sores,
Christ's corpse sags below anguished hands, while
Grief-stricken onlookers faint or kneel in lamentation.

As the sun is setting, before the frontier of memory closes,
I'm seated in a different but familiar garden in Hendesse.   *village north of Heidelberg
Everyone is speaking Pfälzisch, fuzzy and warm,
Except for me and my singsong, faux Bavarian.

Depleted and ravenous, wolfing down
Barnyard-ripe Münsterkäse smeared on   *rich soft cheese from Alsace
Sunflower seed-crusted rye bread,
My friends and I prost our safe return
To Heidelberg, with champagne smuggled,
Along with myself, from the netherworld of France.

Halstead's Bay

With a shiver I recall skating in the moonlight on Halstead's Bay,
Before the first snowfall, when the ice was smooth and thin.
With each stride the clear ice cracked and
The black water rumbled and boomed below.
Fear made me skate faster and faster, seeking the cattailed shore,
Never knowing if I might slide into cold oblivion
Like the nice neighbor lady whose snowmobile fell down a crevasse.
My pleasure in skating at night in late November
Was found in the sheer terror that it made me feel,
Like when I climbed the mast of the yacht I crewed in college
To see if I could glimpse the shoreline through thick Lake Michigan fog.
Mere moments before we struck a jutting pier,
With just feet to spare, with thumping hearts
And arms that flew at the winches, we came about.

*Halstead's Bay = the western-most part of Lake Minnetonka, an early childhood home

Paris

In the light of the January wolf moon
A flotilla of black and white geese glides
Past my house like decoys on a string.

The landscape on both banks of the canal
Blazes with the same pinkish orange that
Flickered over Paris as Notre Dame burned.

The flaming moonlight sparked a vivid dream.
It's the summer of '82 and we're playing tennis
On the sloped red clay of the Jardin du Luxembourg.

Following our game, you lean in for a kiss
And linger long enough for me to caress
Your brawny swimmer's shoulders.

In the next scene, I'm wandering alone
In the treasure-filled sculpture garden
Of Rilke's early workplace, the Musée Rodin.

As I traipse through the Marble Gallery,
You leap out from behind a study for "Eve"
And your smiling cornflower eyes are aglow.

*Wolf moon = full moon associated with the howling of wolves by Native Americans
*Rainer Maria Rilke (1875-1926) = Modernist German poet

Munich

A return to nearly forgotten rituals:
Wishing good morning to rooms full of strangers,
Spreading chopped pork on lye rolls for breakfast,
Writing postcards of the Frauenkirche   *iconic church in the heart of Munich
And animal pictures painted by Franz Marc,
Drinking Weissbier in torch-shaped glasses at any hour of the day,
Spoiling dinner with late afternoon coffee and cake.

During the partial eclipse of the blood moon,
On the banks of the icy River Würm,
I meet German friends, museum people,
Cultured intellectuals of the old school.
A young black cat leaps and dances
Between our feet around a fire-lit picnic.
The stifling heat of the day—
Desert air pulled over the Alps from Africa—
Is quenched by the city's 600 meters of altitude.

The next morning, I visit the jewels of German culture
That somehow survived the Allies' carpet bombing.
A curator friend shows me an old photo of Mary von Stuck
Holding an album with "Adolf Hitler" engraved in gold on the cover.
It is a jolting reminder that the streets and railway platforms of the city
Are the gravestones and tumuli of Munich's deported Jews,
Whose phantoms continue to haunt the sunny beer gardens
Where beautiful unknowing children run and play
With helium-filled unicorns.

*Franz Marc (1880-1916) = prominent German Expressionist painter
*Blood moon = the moon in eclipse appears to be tinted red
*Mary von Stuck (1896-1961) = daughter of the renowned painter and architect Franz von Stuck

Griggstown

Their thirst quenched, the twin fawns scamper
Up the rocky banks of Cider Creek
In pursuit of their mother, a lop-eared doe,
Whose head is cocked forward.

Her eyes of molten onyx scan
The shadow-drenched overgrown border strip
Dividing the blind billionaire's golden, upswept fields
From my neglected, weed-choked lawn.
This is her domain.

Coyotes and foxes are plentiful here,
But the apex predator of young deer
Is the stream of traffic on Canal Road—
Commuter SUVs, lawn-service pickups,
And aspiring Tour-de-France cyclists in racing garb.

In 1777, while still a cart path on
The eastern bank of the Millstone River,
Washington marched his men
Along its bumpy ruts toward Morristown
After the surprise American victory
At the Battle of Princeton.

Cornwallis mounted the opposite shore
On the British retreat to New Brunswick.
Mad to avenge their comrades left splayed
In the blood-smeared mud of Clark's orchard,
The redcoats abducted a local man—Peter van der Veer—
And clubbed him to death.

As twilight falls on Canal Road,
The traffic ebbs to a trickle.
Just footsteps away, on a bend in Cider Creek,
In the zone of unruly vines and lawless ferns,
It is already dark.

The twin fawns, their spots flashing,
Vanish into the hoof prints of their ever-vigilant mother,
Raising clouds of fireflies.

The Coldest Night

With the mercury plunging to fifteen,
The clever birds have fled to their warm roosts.
Frozen to a trickle, the singing stream
No longer flows to the canal, but oozes

Along its curving, stony, steep-sided banks.
The tall jack pines are festooned with garlands
Of frosted moonlight that are gleaming lamps
For the silver deer nibbling in the garden.

Were you here, we would read into the night,
And I would steal hungry glances at your eyes.
Or you might want to keep working, and write—
The room hushed but for Hooksy's lowing sighs.

But I'm here alone with the voiceless fire,
Stoking my ardent mind, flying wings of desire.

Mere Symbols

Last week, in the foggy morning twilight,
In which all colors are shades of grey,
I started walking to the ruined lock house.
It was time to feed the feral black cat.

Heading up Canal Road in the fading darkness,
I nearly trod on the corpses of the twin fawns.
Lying just feet apart, their bodies torn and smashed,
Blood and fur smeared the asphalt in a ghastly gouache.

Just days before Cider Creek had gone completely dry,
Forcing thirsty deer into the nearby stream of traffic—
A deadly blur of shapes, colors, and sounds—
To drink from the canal required a leap into oblivion.

Careless of my sorrow, the bossy slit-eared black tom
Still needed his daily ration of Friskies.
And so, stunned into compliance with old habit,
I stepped over the tiny bodies, still fresh from the kill.

Crossing the center lines obscured by roseate entrails,
I entered the Underworld, the realm of the dead,
Conveyed by a hissing, green-eyed boatman,
Watching from the leaf-strewn banks of the canal.

A few days before I found a cardinal on the ground.
A reckless suicide who flew into my picture window,
His crimson-pink plumage, unnaturally relaxed,
Swirled and furled against my whispered breath.

Stung by the death of a bird I long admired,
The slaughter of the fawns drained my heart's strength.
Blood seeped into my stomach and back up to my mouth,
Where the copper taste made me want to vomit with grief.

This house of river stone and hand-hewn beams,
After six months of labor, is now fully restored.

Stout and warm, is it yet any more tangible or lasting
Than the flight of one of my arrows into the hay bale target?

I want to launch a thousand darts to avenge the fawns,
But who are the enemies I should draw my bow against?
The spooky, circling vultures who will soon be pulling at
The fawns' intestines like ribbons on Christmas presents?

Shall I target the Amazon delivery vans or panzered SUVs?
Or shall I emulate Xerxes—the Persian king,
Who, in impotent fury, lashed the Hellespont—
By lighting the canal ablaze with flaming spears of ire?

This house, my books, my still growing feelings for you—
Are all such protests against our ephemeral selves
Doomed to fly like misfired arrows into the dark woods?
Are any attempts to embody our desires permitted to endure?

If Goethe is right and "mortal things are mere symbols,"
Then how do we become attached to other beings—
Young deer, scarlet birds, and a beloved woman—
With every ounce of our blood and fur?

*Johann Wolfgang von Goethe (1749-1832) = German poet whose line "Alles vergängliche ist nur ein Gleichnis," appears near the end of *Faust, Part Two*

The Morning After

After yesterday's deluge, Cider Creek
Races and overflows its upraised lips.
In the Spring I must not forget to break
Up the swelling dams of vines, leaves, and twigs

That threaten to flood my soggy garden.
Last night the woodpile stacked on the front porch
Fell to the ground, releasing its burden.
The wood was heaped too high, prey to my urge

To create monuments, trophies, and shrines
From the fragments of pictures and feelings,
Theses and projects, coursing through my mind.
How can one curb this drive to make fading

Episodes outlive the passing moment?
Are we not born to read signs and omens?

Voice of the Stars

I wish that I had the voice of the waters,
For then I could sing of your music:
Mentor to the chorusing geese who ply the canal,
Guardian of the little stream that trills even in winter,
Muse of the roaring surf that fills our ears with oblivion,
Your night murmurs form the melody I hear in my dreams.

I wish that I had the voice of Artemis,
For then I could sing of your beauty:
Leonine shoulders somehow borne by your lithe frame,
Fox-footed fingertips whose soft touch lingers on the skin,
Lupine irises that change color with the light or your mood,
Your face is the image that I hold in my heart.

I wish that I had the voice of the stars,
For then I could sing of your ancestry:
Daughter of the half-darkened sun and the waxing moon,
Sister of lightning strikes and the green-patinaed aurora,
Mistress of Orion, Polaris, and the Great She-Bear,
Your eyes are meteors that emblazon the dark sky.

*Artemis = Greek goddess of the hunt, wild animals, and the moon
*Orion = constellation named after a legendary hunter in Greek mythology
*Polaris = the North Star which is found in the constellation Ursa Minor (Lesser She-Bear)
*Great She-Bear = Ursa Major, a constellation in the northern sky

Heart Poem

On another grey morning after
The sun set the earth afire,
My sick heart is my jailor.

I can't translate Nietzsche,
Or cycle on the towpath,
Or venture out to see you.

The utmost of permitted tasks
Is to feed my ungrateful charge,
The feral black tomcat.

Then, before sorrow ruined the day,
A solitary doe found her way
Into my back garden.

With uncanny grace she leapt the fence
And ambled over to the apples
Put out with the birdseed.

Her pleasure in the sweet fruit
Banished my joyless self-pity
And vexing heartache.

Alone and hoping to be found,
I willed her to edge close enough
To caress her velvet flanks.

Time Poem

It doesn't seem to matter how willing we are,
The river of time between us is ever widening.

Last week in Brooklyn, the meeting of
Our eyes turned us both into statues,
Rigid and aloof, like the chiseled grey deer
Standing stock still in my garden at twilight.

We are unknown to one another now,
Having forgotten how the faintest touch,
Just one word, back then, moved us so.

Those precious months we spent together
Is a sandbar vanishing under a rising tide.
Soon we'll have no choice but to jump back
To the beach, to solid ground, before we drown.

Birth Poem

The birth of feeling, of feeling deeply for another,
For the world of beauty and the poems of our youth,
Is fed by the cold March rain that stirs
The doves to nest and the flowers to bloom.

The feelings being born must pass through the scars that grew
In the time of forgetting, the murder of lions, and the burying of the self
In the pain of others too absorbed in suffering to know
Whose lives and loves were subsumed in their sorrow.

To reach this peak, this pinnacle of feeling, is
To walk the path toward the source of one's fears,
Toward one's desires, to discover what one needs,
To miss your presence in all the corners of my life.

Pinecone Poem

On the morning after snow, hail, and rain,
The sunrise breaks through a prim horizon.
A corona of ripe clementine seeps
Upwards before melding with the blue sky.

Prior to leaving for the hospital, I threw
The week-old irises—with inward-curling lips—
Onto the compost heap just past the new woodpile
That lies near the rude plank bridge over the singing stream.

Squirrels hunch on the bridge to husk walnuts,
Leaving piles of coal black rind on the boards.
Countless generations have filled their treetop nests
And seeded the creek banks with a palisade of saplings.

Overnight, in the storm winds, the female jack pines
Shed dozens of pinecones over the gravel drive.
These perfect objects, so intricately designed,
Make me proleptically mourn my much-loved life.

Stolen Dog

Awaking from heart surgery, I panicked
That I could not find some precious things:
Beloved books with notes in the margins,
My Heidelberg diaries written with a fountain pen
On cheap checkered paper bound in red,
Tickets to a concert I could not bear to miss,
And a favorite childhood dog who was stolen by boat
From our house on a lake in the woods.
A Samoyed, he was snow white,
With black-rimmed eyes, a smiling mouth, and
A tail that curled over his back.
For years afterwards, on every car trip, I looked for him,
Examining every dog we happened to pass,
For his black-rimmed eyes and smiling mouth.

Tree Shadows

As Cider Creek purls and daffodils
Are breaking through its stony banks,
The deer enter the garden. They gather
Around the saltlick and trail of horse oats
Where their angular shapes merge with the
Tree shadows cast by the midday sun.

Having daintily browsed their fill,
They are tender to one another,
Nuzzling and being nuzzled,
Grooming and being groomed.
Even when startled, they are precise
And graceful in all their movements.

The yearling fawns are still playful,
Bucking and cantering in circles
Around their mothers. The smallest one,
However, still refuses to jump the fence.
Scouting out a gap in the rotting rails,
She pokes her mouse-grey head through.

I long to stroke her silken ears and
Peer into her eyes of liquid blackness.
But surely, she would shy away from me
And spring swiftly into the dark woods,
Leaving me to ponder when and where
I shall ever feel so entirely alive again.

Gregory Maertz is a professor of English at St. John's University in New York City, where he teaches courses on Romanticism and Fascism Studies. He studied languages and literature at Northwestern, Georgetown, and Heidelberg, and earned his graduate degrees at Harvard. His scholarly books include *Children of Prometheus: Romanticism and Its Legacy* (2021), *Nostalgia for the Future: Modernism and Heterogeneity in the Visual Arts of Nazi Germany* (2019), *Literature and the Cult of Personality: Essays on Goethe and His Influence* (2017), which are available from Columbia University Press, and critical editions of George Eliot's *Middlemarch* and Friedrich Nietzsche's *On the Genealogy of Morality* (both published by Broadview Press). In addition, he has curated exhibitions in Berlin and Bergen, Norway, on the art of the Third Reich. Maertz's research on literature and art has been supported by major grants from the NEH, the ACLS, the National Humanities Center, the Gerda Henkel Stiftung, CASVA at the National Gallery of Art, and the Institute for Advanced Study in Princeton. He has held visiting positions at Washington University in St. Louis and Duke.

The Charisma of Animals is Maertz's first volume of verse. Completed during the first two years of the COVID-19 pandemic, the poems presented here incorporate structural and sonic echoes of formalism in brief lyrics and longer narratives which seek to make transient, intensely personal experiences—love and loss, illness and recovery, encounters with nature and animals as well as history and works of art—concrete and accessible. They belong to the province of sensations, memories, dreams, and sacred places in Maertz's personal mythology: the fishing village of Gravir in the Outer Hebrides (home of Eriskay ponies, the eponymous white horses), the Hawaiian Islands, Lake Minnetonka, Manhattan, Heidelberg, Munich, Bergen, Paris, and Griggstown, an historic village on the outskirts of Princeton, New Jersey, where he makes his home with Hooksy, a big orange tabby, in a former cidery.

www.ingramcontent.com/pod-product-compliance
Lightning Source LLC
Chambersburg PA
CBHW020934180426
43192CB00036B/1144